# JUST BELIEVE

## Dwayne Norman

Empyrion Publishing
PO Box 784327
Winter Garden FL 34778

*Just Believe*

Copyright © 2015 by Dwayne Norman

ISBN: 978-0692374634

Empyrion Publishing
PO Box 784327
Winter Garden FL 34778
info@EmpyrionPublishing.com

Unless otherwise noted, all Scripture quotations are from the New King James Version of the Bible.

*Printed in the United States of America*

# CONTENTS

# CHAPTER
# 1

# THE SPIRIT OF FAITH

I heard a great teacher of faith give this response when asked why he taught so much about faith. He said according to Ephesians 2:8 we are <u>saved</u> by faith. No one can be saved without faith! Romans 1:17 says the just shall <u>live</u> by faith. As Christians (who got saved by faith) we cannot live without faith! The Bible says that we <u>walk</u> by faith (II Corinthians 5:7). We can't walk with God everyday if we don't have faith! II Thessalonians 1:3 tells us we <u>grow</u> (spiritually) by faith. The Apostle Paul said your faith grows exceedingly. And according to Hebrews 11:6, it is impossible to please God without faith. God said it is impossible! You and I cannot please our Father God without faith! So, we are saved, we walk, we live, we grow and we please God by faith. It sounds to me like faith is very, very important. Of course it's not the only subject to teach from the Bible, but it is one we should <u>major in</u>!

Do you remember the story in Mark 9:14-27 where a father brought his son to Jesus?  He wanted the Lord to cast the demon out of his child.  When they came to Jesus, the spirit in the boy convulsed him and he fell to the ground and wallowed, foaming at the mouth. Verses 21-23 says:

**"So He asked his father, "How long has this been happening to him?"  And he said, "From childhood.**

**"And often he has thrown him both into the fire and into the water to destroy him.  But if You can do anything, have compassion on us and help us."**

**Jesus said to him, "If you can believe, all things are possible to him who believes.""**

I like this story because it reminds me of what many of us have done when coming to the Lord for help.  The father said, "...If you can do anything..."  In other words he wanted to put the responsibility for the deliverance of his son on Jesus.  Many of us have done the same thing.  We have come to God and said, "God, if you are really all powerful then do something about my kids, my marriage, my job, my finances or my situation."  It did not occur to us that there was something we needed to do first.  It did not occur to us that maybe we have a responsibility we have not fulfilled.  This man came to Jesus for help.  He put the ball (so to speak) in Jesus' lap, but look what Jesus did with the ball.  He put it back in the man's lap.

He said if you can believe, then all things (including what you need for your son) will be possible for you.  Let me paraphrase it this way. The Lord could have said, "I know I am all powerful and I can do all things, but you must believe or operate in faith to activate my power to work on your behalf." We must believe first, and then God will move on our behalf! Many want to believe God after they see Him work in their situation, but if God worked that way you would not need to have faith; because it would already be done. We believe first, God's power is released and our miracle comes. Just because God is omnipotent doesn't mean His power will be automatically released into our lives to change our situations. A great minister from years ago said that God would skip over a million needy people just to get to one person who believes. It's not our need that God responds to any more, it's our faith. If you never believe God for your healing, you will maintain a need for healing all of your life and never be healed. To have your need for healing met, you must believe you receive your healing before you see or feel it; that's the way of faith. God responded to our need once and for all at Calvary. He answered the need of all humanity when Jesus came and suffered, died and arose from the dead. That was when God met the need of the entire human race for eternity.

Now, to experience what God did for us in Christ, we must operate in faith! We all must believe God so He can manifest in the natural realm what He already did for us in Christ at Calvary. What does that mean? Well, let me say it this way. If you want to feel and see your healing you still have to receive it by faith, even though God already healed you through the 39 stripes of Jesus almost 2000 years ago. That is why so many Christians never get healed or experience their healing; it's not an automatic thing. The same is true in being born-again. Jesus obtained salvation for all of humanity, but it's not an automatic thing. A lost person will only experience salvation when he believes or has faith in what Jesus did for him at Calvary. Jesus obtained forgiveness of sin and eternal life for all humanity, but every individual person must receive by faith what God accomplished for him (Romans 10:9, 10). The same is true for healing, finances, joy, peace and whatever we need from God. Our needs were met through Jesus' shed Blood at the cross, but we still must believe, to appropriate them or experience them being met. All that God finished for us in Christ will not automatically materialize in our lives. Even though the Lord finished everything for us, and is now offering all these blessings to us as free gifts from His grace, <u>we</u> still have a part or responsibility in this. We must spiritually reach out with our faith and take what He is offering us. If we don't take it by faith, we will not experience it. If we don't experience what the Lord has already done for us in Christ, then don't blame the Lord for that, because it's not His fault! It's our fault! The only way to receive from God's abundant grace is by faith (Romans 4:16)!

Look with me at verses 18 & 19.

**"And wherever it seizes him, it throws him down; he foams at the mouth, gnashes his teeth, and becomes rigid. So I spoke to Your disciples that they should cast it out, but they <u>could not</u>."**

**He answered him and said, "O faithless generation, how long shall I be with you?  How long shall I bear with you?  Bring him to Me.""**

If you have read our book "How to Respond to a Bad Report" you will see that I am reiterating some things I said in that book.  It bears repeating because both of these books are about using our faith.  I may use a few of the Scriptures from the other book, but I also want to share with you some other things from those Scriptures I did not bring out before; so we might say this book is part 2 of "How To Respond to a Bad Report".   Either way, we need to keep reading and hearing the Word over and over again.  We will never hear it too much!  Therefore, if you notice in verse 18, the father said the disciples <u>could not</u> cast the demon out of the boy.  That implies they did not have the power to cast the demon out, and that was not correct.  In Luke 9:1, Jesus gave His disciples authority and power over <u>ALL</u> demons, which would include this one.  If it was from a lack of power, Jesus would have said, "O <u>powerless</u> generation; instead of faithless generation."  The Lord knew exactly what happened here.  Matthew's account, chapter 17, verses 19, 20 says:

**"Then the disciples came to Jesus privately and said, "Why could we not cast it out?"
So Jesus said to them, "Because of your unbelief…""**

He did not say because of your lack of power.  He said the disciples were in unbelief; therefore the power of

God was there, but it was not activated to drive the demon out. Obviously the demon manifested himself through the boy in such a way as to trick the disciples in turning their faith off, and it worked. But if you read the rest of the story, he tried the same thing on Jesus, but it did not work on Him. Jesus kept His faith applied which activated God's power to make the demon leave. Always keep your faith in God and your eyes on Jesus, and don't be moved by what the devil does. Satan is defeated, and we have all authority and power over him in Jesus Name!

Again, the father of the boy expected Jesus to do something about his problem, but he didn't realize there was something he needed to do first. Let's say I decide to iron my shirt at 8 in the morning, but I never plug the iron in the wall socket. Then let's say you come over about 9PM and see me standing right next to the wall socket (where all the power is) holding the iron and its plug in my hands. What would you say? Maybe, "Why didn't you iron your shirt?" I respond, "The iron never got hot." You would probably look at me and think, "No one can be that dumb!" Even though I knew there was plenty of power in the wall, just standing close as I could to the wall socket would not heat up the iron. I still had to make a connection with that power. I still had to plug the iron in the wall to activate the power that was already there.

You could be dying from some terrible disease and Jesus could appear to you in your living room. He could stand right in front of you, with all power to heal, and yet you could still die from that disease. Just being close to where the power is does not activate it. Just holding a stick of dynamite in your hand doesn't cause it to explode; you must lite the fuse. If you think about it, God's power is everywhere, because He is everywhere. His power is in every home, in every hospital and place of business, but it doesn't automatically flow and produce miracles for people unless they learn how to tap into it. The spiritual plug we use to tap into God's power is our faith. We must make that connection to experience what we need from the Lord. If we don't learn how to use our faith, it will be like going day after day holding our iron in our hands wondering why it will not get hot.

Jesus was telling the boy's father that to tap into God's power to do the impossible you must believe. Many times Jesus told people that their need would be met according to <u>their faith</u>. He never told anyone he would be healed according to His (meaning Jesus) faith. Jesus never told anyone, "I have perfect faith, therefore you will be healed." As Believers, we need to get a hold of this! The Lord said all things are possible to him who believes! Wow! Just believe! Someone said, "It can't be that simple." I didn't say this. Jesus said it, and He cannot lie (Numbers 23:19; Tutus1:2)! Think about that! That's a huge statement! If we would learn how to operate in faith, everything would be possible for us! The Lord made it very simple, but man has made it very complex. Let's get back to the simplicity of believing.

So, what does it mean to operate in faith or to believe God? If you were to ask many Christians, "How do you know you are in faith for your healing, peace, finances, etc..?" Most of the time there answers would be a litany of their good works. Many would say, "I know I am in faith because I go to church 3 times a week, give my tithes, read 5 chapters out of my Bible every day, pray 2 hours a day and give to support the unwed mother's home." All of these good works are very important and God will bless you for doing them, but that doesn't mean you are in faith for your healing. Please understand this! As important as good works are, we cannot earn our healing by doing them; yet many Believers have thought that very way. If the manifestation of our healing is delayed in coming to pass, it usually raises a question in our minds, "I am a good Christian, and I am serving the Lord. Why hasn't He brought my healing to pass?" Even if we don't express this type of thought to others, we are still basing our healing on good works and not faith. The devil has deceived many Christians this way, and many of them have come to the false conclusion that God does not want them healed. Yes it's true that God will reward and bless us for our good works and faithfulness to serve Him, and it pleases Him very much, but that is not why we can be healed. If you are faithful to do everything God tells you to, but you don't believe that by Jesus' stripes you are healed; then you will probably not be healed. If someone asked you why you are in faith for your healing, your answer should be something like this, "Because I believe God's Word! I believe that by the stripes of Jesus I am healed! And I believe that my healing will come to pass in my body in Jesus' Name!"

Jesus didn't tell the boy's father, "All things are possible to him who goes to church a lot, prays a lot and reads the Bible a lot." Again, those things are very important, but we receive healing by faith freely from God's grace. Christians have proven over the centuries that you can do all these good things and remain sick, broke and depressed all of your life. It's very important that we go to church, pray, read our Bibles and live a holy life, but the only way to receive from God is by faith; our faith. Not by our spouses faith, or our pastor's faith, or our neighbor's faith or the faith of the priest! Remember, Jesus told the woman with the issue of blood that her (not Jesus' faith) faith made her well. Yes, Jesus healed her, but it was because her faith activated His healing power to go into her body and make her whole. If you read that story in Mark 5, you will see that many people were touching Jesus, but she was the only one He responded to for healing. Some people act like Jesus is a big spiritual rabbit's foot, if they could just rub Him or touch Him then something miraculous might happen to them. No, no, no! If we touch Him with our faith, then we can expect something miraculous to happen to us! And that is what Jesus was encouraging the father to do for his son. (Mark 9:24-27)

**"Immediately the father of the child cried out and said with tears, "Lord, I believe; help my unbelief!"**
**When Jesus saw that the people came running together, He rebuked the unclean spirit, saying to it: "Deaf and dumb spirit, I command you, come out of him and enter him not more!"**

**Then the spirit cried out, convulsed him greatly, and came out of him. And he became as one dead, so that many said, "He is dead."**

**But Jesus took him by the hand and lifted him up, and he arose."**

The Lord did not tell the father he had to have a degree in theology or any other requirements before he could believe. It was just that simple. Jesus said all things are possible to him who believes. So, let's not add anything to that. Let's get back to what the Bible says and not what man's religion says. Listen to what the Apostle Paul said in II Corinthians 4:13:

**"And since we have the same spirit of faith, according to what is written, "I believed and therefore I spoke," we also believe and therefore speak."**

If you notice, he did not say since we all have the same faith. He said since we all have the same <u>spirit</u> of faith. I believe there is a difference. It's true. We do have the same faith even though we may not be using it like we should. When I say we (Christians) have the same faith, I mean the same kind of faith. The Apostle Peter, writing to Believers in II Peter 1:1 said, **"Simon Peter, a bondservant and apostle of Jesus Christ, to those who have obtained <u>like</u> precious faith with us by the righteousness of our God and Savior Jesus Christ."** The margin of my Bible says that the word "like" means faith of the same value. We have the same kind of faith because our faith is from the same source. Hebrews

12:2 tells us that Jesus is the author and developer of our faith. Well, since Jesus is God, and He authored our faith; what kind of faith would we have? The God kind. To say you have the God kind of faith doesn't mean you just joined a specific movement; it simply means you believe the Bible. I can't give any one faith, but if I could, then that person would have the Dwayne Norman kind of faith. Since God is the originator of our faith, then the only kind we could have would be His kind. We all got our faith from God so the only kind we could have would be the God kind. Now, just because every Believer has a measure of God's faith (Romans 12:3; Ephesians 2:8; Hebrews 12:2; James 2:1) doesn't mean he will automatically start seeing lots of miracles. There is a difference between having faith and using it. Look what the Lord said in Matthew 21:21.

**"So Jesus answered and said to them, "Assuredly, I say to you, <u>If you have</u> <u>faith and do not doubt</u>, you will not only do what was done to the fig tree, but also if you say to this mountain, 'Be removed and be cast into the sea,' it will be done."**

I want you to pay close attention in that verse to the phrase "if you have faith and do not doubt". He could have just said, "...if you have faith, you will not only do what was done to the fig tree..." but He did not. The Lord said two different things here. He said you must have faith and you must not doubt. By saying you must not doubt, tells us that just having a measure of faith is not enough; in other words, we must release or use it.

Not doubting implies using your faith. Let me give you an example. I have a lawn mower at home, but that doesn't mean my yard will get mowed. So, what if I made this statement, "If you have a lawn mower your yard will get mowed?" Would that be accurate? Would just having a lawn mower guarantee your yard would be mowed? No. What if I said it this way? If you have a lawn mower and will use it, your yard will get mowed. That sounds better doesn't it? That is what Jesus meant when He said if you have faith and do not doubt. You can have faith (because it's a free gift from God) and allow it to be inactive, like having a lawn mower in your shed that you have not used for years.

An equivalent verse to what we are talking about is James 2:14, "What does it profit, my brethren, if someone says he has faith but does not have works? Can faith save him?" To reiterate, if you have a lawn mower and won't use it, will your yard get mowed? Your faith will not get you healed if you will not use it or put it to work. It is through the work of faith that God's power is activated (II Thessalonians 1:11).

Again, when Jesus said do not doubt, He was saying you must believe that the things you say will come to pass, then you will have what you say (Mark 11:23). The Apostle Paul said that we don't just have the same faith, but we have the same <u>spirit</u> of faith. He said to have the same spirit of faith means to believe that what you say will come to pass. For me, the phrase "spirit of faith" implies faith in action; whereas, just having faith implies that you have something, but you are not using it. Also, he didn't say that anything you confess would be manifested! He did not say that the only thing necessary is what you say. The condition is, you <u>must believe</u> that what you say will be manifested before it is, and then it will come to pass. That is the spirit of faith we need working in our lives every day! Just having a lawn mower in our shed doesn't mean the yard will get mowed. Remember, the power of God will only be activated to produce results for us when we release or operate in faith. So, if we want to see God's power working for us and through us for others, let's get developed in operating in the spirit of faith!

Some Christians have gotten in trouble though after hearing a good faith message. As soon as they learned that God gave them a measure of faith, they thought they could start confessing or believe for anything right then; and it doesn't work that way. Faith is just like a muscle in our bodies, it must be developed. It is possible to be a "muscle man", but that will not come over night.

What Jesus said to us is true. All things are possible to him who believes. Jesus was explaining the potential available to us through our faith in God. But our same Bible tells us that we are to grow in faith, and that faith comes by hearing God's Word (Romans 10:17; II Thessalonians 1:3).

God gave us a measure of faith when we got saved, but it did not come fully developed. If you have not learned that yet, you need to. Even though it is possible to believe God for a new house, you may not want to start there for your first act of faith. You might start with believing God for a pair of shoes, then go on to bigger things. Don't stretch your faith so far out that you will get discouraged and give up before your miracle comes to pass. If you have never bench pressed 75 lbs. you may not want to start with 500 lbs. Yes, it may be possible for you to bench press 500 lbs. but you will not do it over night. That is why you can't just say anything and see it come to pass. You must <u>believe</u> that what you say will be done, and you will not believe that if your faith is not developed to that level.

If you are confessing for $1,000,000 and have never used your faith for $100, then what you are confessing (no matter how many times you say it) will not come to pass; because you are not in faith. Yes, you have a measure of faith, but it's not developed to believe God for $1,000,000 yet. You are over loading your faith! Your faith in your heart is not developed to the place where it is in agreement with the words coming out of your mouth. You <u>must truly believe</u> that what you say will come to pass, or it won't! Now let me say this also. It's true that God wants us to use our faith for the things we need, but more importantly, let's use our faith to believe God to win more lost people to Jesus, to see more people healed and delivered, and to finance the Gospel into every nation! So, don't just endeavor to have strong faith so you can get all the "things" you want.

Again remember, II Corinthians 4:13. Paul said it was the same spirit of faith that <u>believes</u> and <u>speaks</u>. Even though we all have the same kind of faith, we may not be believing or saying anything. Faith is an act! It's not passive! When we start believing God's Word and speaking it, we start operating in the same spirit of faith. When we believe I Peter 2:24, by Jesus's stripes we are healed, and start saying it, we are now operating in the same spirit of faith.  You have to <u>believe</u> and <u>say.</u>  The Apostle Paul did not say that we must believe that God will say it for us.  He said we <u>must believe what we say</u>. The Lord Jesus said if <u>we</u> <u>believe</u> that the things <u>we</u> <u>say</u> will be done; then we will have what we say!  If you are having problems with your knee and you believe that by Jesus' stripes you are healed, then speak to your knee and command it to function normally in Jesus' Name! Start moving your leg and thank the Lord Jesus that your knee is healed. Even if it doesn't feel healed, begin to thank the Lord that it is in Jesus' Name!  The same spirit of faith believes and says.

*Just Believe*

# CHAPTER
2

# BREATHING AND BELIEVING

No matter how simple God makes things, there will always be people who will try to make them complex. God made believing very simple, let's not make it difficult. Believing is just a choice we make. Faith is just a choice or decision we make. We choose to believe or not to believe. God has given us hundreds of promises from His Word, and He cannot lie. Now it's our turn to do something, we either choose to believe His Word or we don't. It doesn't take 3 months to choose to believe God's Word. What are you waiting on? It's just a decision. Faith is just a decision. You can choose right now to believe that by Jesus' stripes you are healed. If you want to wait 3 months to believe that, you can, but it will not make God's Word any truer. Hebrews 4:2, 3 says:

**"For indeed the gospel was preached to us as well as to them; but <u>the word</u> which <u>they heard</u> did not profit them, <u>not being mixed with faith</u> in those who heard it. For we who have believed do enter that rest..."**

The Bible says that faith comes by hearing God's Word. These people heard the Word, but they did not automatically believe that Word. If was up to them to mix the Word they heard with faith. Even though they heard it, they still had to make a decision to believe it. That means we can hear the Word all day and choose not to believe it, and it will not do us any good. We are the mixer. We must mix the Word we hear with faith, by making a decision to believe it as we hear it and read it. Also, no one can stand in the gap for me and mix faith with the Word I hear. I have to do the mixing. I have to make a decision to believe, no one else can make that decision for me.

God has really been impressing on me that we need to get back to the simplicity of believing. Once again, what does it mean to believe? How long does it take to believe something? Do you have to know everything about a matter before you can believe? If a friend of mine brought a chair over to my house and asked me to sit in it, I would have to make a decision on whether I would do that or not. I might ask him a few questions about the chair, but it would not take me 3 months before I decided to sit down in it. I would make a decision right then, either I believe it's ok or I don't. Believing is a decision of my will. When I heard the Gospel of salvation, faith came to me to get saved

(Romans 10:9, 17). I did not have to know the whole Bible or everything about Jesus before I could make a decision to believe in Him. It was something I did very quickly because I chose to. Therefore, to release your faith concerning a matter is not something that has to take 6 months. You can decide to believe something immediately. When you read God's Word, you can decide right then if you believe it. It's that simple. It's your choice. You don't need a week to decide if you believe what you read in the Bible. You can decide as soon as you read it. That is how simple it is to make a decision to believe.

When I talk about the simplicity of believing, I am talking about how quickly one can make a decision to believe or not to believe. Even though we still need to develop our faith, it doesn't take long to make a decision as to whether we believe something or not. If you are sick and I ask you if you believe that by Jesus' stripes you are healed, right then you can say, "I believe that or I don't believe that." You won't need to say, "I will have to get back with you on that in about 3 months." You can decide right then which way you believe. If you know you don't believe you are healed, then you need to confess and read those verses on healing until you can honestly say, "I believe by Jesus' stripes I am healed." But once you make the decision to believe that it is done for you, then stand your ground and praise the Lord until it comes to pass, that is, until you can see it and feel it. Therefore, once you read or hear God's Word about something He has done for you in Christ, you can decide right then if you believe it or not.

We all need to practice using our faith; we may find that we can already believe God for more than we thought we could.  In studying the ministry of Jesus, I have noticed that He told people that their healing would come to pass according to their faith.  There is not one place in the four Gospels where He ever told anyone to go and meditate the Word for two weeks and then come back and see Him.  I know that Jesus ministered under a very strong anointing, but most of the time the people still received by their faith.  Their faith activated the healing power in Jesus.  He never told anyone go to Bible school first, before He would minister to them.  He never told anyone to get a degree in theology before God's power could be activated.  Of course the Bible is filled with Scriptures on how vital it is for Believers to study, meditate and confess God's Word to grow strong in the Lord, which is part of Jesus' command to go and teach and make disciples of all the nations.  Those things are very important, but right now you may be able to believe God for more than you realize if you would just make the decision to step out in faith on His Word!  Now God can't lie, so whether you believe or not, will not change the truth of His Word (Romans 3:4).  In our book, "God's Will is Healing for Everyone", I talked some about Jesus healing the leper in Mark 1:40-42. I want you to see something else from that story.

**"Now a leper came to Him, imploring Him, kneeling down to Him and saying to Him, "If You are willing, You can make me clean.""**

**Then Jesus, moved with compassion, stretched out His hand and touched him, and said to him, "I am willing; be cleansed."**

**<u>As soon as He had spoken</u>, immediately the leprosy left him, and he was cleansed."**

If you notice in these verses, the leper wasn't healed until after Jesus had spoken. The Bible says the Lord reached out and touched the man and said He was willing to heal him. Even though He laid hands on the man before He said this, it was still after Jesus had spoken that the man was healed. The man could not release or operate in faith until God's will for healing was revealed to him. In other words, he could not make a decision to believe God for his healing until he knew God's will. God's Word is His will to us. As one minister said years ago, "Faith can only be released where the will of God is known." We must be convinced that God wants us healed, or we will not believe it in our hearts and confess it with our mouths. What I especially wanted you to see was how quickly the leper made the decision to believe. It didn't take him 3 months, did it? His leprosy left immediately after Jesus spoke to him. That means he made a decision to believe immediately after he heard what the will of God was. Obviously, he was not operating in faith before the Lord spoke to him or he would have been healed, but when God's will was made known to him, he quickly stepped out in faith and received. You and I can do the same thing! Again, the leper did not have to do anything else before he could believe, and you don't either. When you read God's

Word <u>just believe</u> and obey it; it's your choice! What will be your decision?

We don't have to squint our eyes real tight or pray in tongues as hard and fast as we can to believe God. It is not about physically trying to work up anything or hyping up ourselves. Let's just simply believe what God says. **<u>The spirit of faith is a demonstration of the simplicity of believing</u>.** Let's get back to that! Kenneth Hagin Sr. always taught us that the epistles are the letters written from God to the Church. He taught us that Christians are Believers, and the reason we are called Believers is because we believe. We believe in Jesus as our Lord and Savior. We believe the Word of God. We believe that God cannot lie and He watches over His Word to perform it (Jeremiah 1:12; Numbers 23:19)!

Brother Hagin said that when you read the epistles you will notice there are not any Scriptures that encourage Believers to believe. I am not aware of any Scriptures that say as a Believer you need to believe. That would be like saying as a human being you need to breathe. There are some verses, like II Corinthians 4:13, that teach us what the spirit of faith is, what it means to believe God and how important our faith is, but the Lord really doesn't come out and tell Believers they are supposed to believe. Our question now should be, "Why not?" I have noticed that many Christians get into a mode or rut of <u>trying</u> to believe. They struggle, as though it is something difficult to do, and it should not be that way. It should be easy to believe God! We should have fun believing God! As Believers that's what we do, that is our spiritual nature. It should be perfectly normal for us to believe God's Word, and to believe that what we confess from His Word will come to pass in our lives! That should be the norm in the life of every Christian! I think all of us should return to normal Christianity! But what is that? That means believing the Bible and doing it! Now the world will consider us abnormal, but they are the ones abnormal. You can't be normal (or the way God created you to be) if you talk and live your life contrary to the principles of God's Word! The world (of unbelievers-those who are not born again) does not live in the same kingdom as Christians. They think we are strange because our kingdom operates by the laws of faith and love. They don't understand that, and they never will until they get saved.

If you think about it, believing God should be just as easy as breathing. Breathing is not something foreign to me. It is not difficult at all! It is not something that I struggle with every day! It is not something I try to do! Why? Because it's my nature to breathe! That is what I naturally do. I do not need my friends to call me every day to encourage me to breathe! I do not need someone to write a book that encourages human beings to breathe! I don't get up each day and go straight to my refrigerator to look at the paper I posted on the door. It says, "Seven things to do if you want to breathe." I don't need to do that, do you? I go to bed breathing and I get up breathing. I really don't think about it, do you? Spiritually it should be the same way as a Believer. Physically I live by breathing. Spiritually I live by believing. Believing what? Believing God and His Word, and believing that the things I say will come to pass (Mark 11:23). I don't need my friends to call me and remind me to believe, that should be supernaturally natural. Believing God should be as normal to me as breathing. It should not be frustrating or something I struggle to do!

Jesus told the father in Mark 9:23, **"If you can believe, all things are possible to him who believes."** He said if you can believe. What if He said if you can breathe? You would not have to think about that, would you? You would not tell the Lord to give you three days to get back with Him on that would you? As a human being, breathing is what you do. Well, as a Believer, believing is what you do. If Jesus appeared to you and said, "If you can believe...", you should quickly say, "I can, because that is what I do. I'm a Believer." Every day as a person, I breathe. Every day as a Believer, I believe.

As a Christian, if I said to you, "Just breathe", you would very simply say, "OK". And so, if I say to you, "Just believe", you should very simply say, "OK". But what many Believers say is, "I'm really trying. I'm trying my best but it's so hard." If they responded the same way about breathing (with the exception of having some kind of lung disease) we would not think that was normal. If your friend said, "I am trying my best to breathe every day", you would assume he has some type of breathing problem, because that would not be a normal thing to say. Spiritually, it's not normal for Believers to say they are trying to believe. That is why we are Believers because we believe God! We don't try to breathe, we just do it! We don't try to believe God, we just do it! As soon as we were born, we started breathing. As soon as we were spiritually born, we started believing. Yes, we need to develop our faith to believe God for greater things for His glory, but we can still believe God every day on whatever spiritual level we are presently at.

If by chance you are thinking that your faith isn't developed enough right now to produce anything then look with me at what the Apostle Paul said to the Christians in Galatians 3:1-3.

**"O foolish Galatians! Who has bewitched you that you should not obey the truth, before whose eyes Jesus Christ was clearly portrayed among you as crucified?**

**This only I want to learn from you: Did you receive the Spirit by the works of the law, or by the hearing of faith?**

**Are you so foolish? Having begun in the Spirit, are you now being made perfect by the flesh?**

Let me remind you that to walk in the Spirit, you must walk by faith, and to walk by faith means your faith is developed enough to do that. To walk in the Spirit really means to walk and live out of your reborn spirit, led by the Holy Spirit. Therefore, to walk in the Spirit every day, you must walk by faith, which means you must believe and obey God's Word. But what I want you to see is that Paul told these Believers that they began doing that the moment they received Jesus into their hearts. They initially began walking in the Spirit at the moment of their salvation. The biggest and greatest miracle is the new birth (passing from spiritual death to spiritual life). Now, think about how easy it is to become a Christian. All a lost person needs to do is to confess Jesus as his Lord and Savior, and believe that God raised Him from the dead (Romans 10:9). All he did was to hear the Gospel and make a decision to believe it.

That means when you were the most spiritually ignorant you would ever be, you were able to operate in faith and receive the greatest miracle there is! Meditate on that for a minute. It was very obvious that you did not understand then, all that you understand now about faith. My point is, even though we need to continually grow in faith, it seems that anything else we will ever need in life should be easier to receive, since we have already received the greatest of all miracles! Again, when we knew the least about God, we were able to believe and receive the greatest blessing He has given the human race! Wow! Is it any wonder Jesus said that all things are possible to him who believes (Mark 9:23)! We have already received God's biggest blessing, so why should we struggle with anything else. Look with me at how quickly a lame man believed God for his healing in Acts 14:8-10.

**"And in Lystra a certain man without strength in his feet was sitting, a cripple from his mother's womb, who had never walked.**
**This man heard Paul speaking, Paul, observing him intently and seeing that <u>he had faith to be healed</u>.**

**Said with a loud voice, "Stand up straight on your feet!" And he leaped and walked."**

This man had never walked, so this was a great healing-miracle! And look how fast the man was able to believe God for his healing. Since this is the only record we have of this man's healing, we must assume this was the first time he heard the message of faith for healing (Paul said that he preached the word of faith - Romans 10:8). It did not say the lame man studied the healing Scriptures for 2 years before he heard Paul's message. Again, the Bible tells us that we definitely need to study to show ourselves approved, but I also believe that our faith is much stronger, right now, than we realize. If we would make a decision, like this man at Lystra did, to believe the Word we hear, and act on it, then we would see what our faith in God can do. At least it would help us to locate our level of faith. Like I said, that was probably the first time this lame man had ever heard the Word (faith comes by hearing the Word), and when he did, that Word for healing went right into his spirit. Right then he made a decision to believe that healing was for him, and Paul knew it. He was immediately healed! That shows me that it doesn't always have to take a long time for our faith to be developed for what we would consider a great miracle.

I want to show you some other things the Lord Jesus said about believing. In John 6:47, He said, **"Most assuredly, I say to you, he who <u>believes</u> in Me <u>has</u> everlasting life."** What He was actually saying was, **"He who believes has."** What does he have? Whatever he is believing God for.  How do you have to believe in Jesus to have everlasting life?  You have to believe in Him as your Savior.  If you believe in Him as your healer, you have healing.  If you believe in Him as your provider, you have provision or prosperity.  The whole point is, if you believe, you have.  The Lord said, in Matthew 7:8, **"For everyone who <u>asks receives</u>, and he who <u>seeks finds</u>, and to him who knocks it will be opened."**  I like the way Smith Wigglesworth said this.  He said, "Asking, therefore, is receiving, and seeking is finding."  You may need to stop and think about that for a couple of minutes, so that it can soak in.  Jesus did not say if you ask, you might receive.  If you seek, you might find.  By saying asking is receiving, the Lord was saying that if we truly ask correctly (in faith, believing) then it's as good as done.  You don't have to wonder if you will receive the manifestation of your answer.  As far as you are concerned, your prayer is answered.  You need to believe that seeking <u>is</u> finding.  If you seek God correctly (In faith, believing.  Seeking Him in line with His Word, which is His will for you), then you have found.  Believe that and expect it to come to pass!

Now, let's add in here what we read over in John, Chapter 6.  Whoever believes, has.  Jesus did not say if you believe you might have salvation, healing, prosperity, etc...  He said if you believe, you have.  Therefore, I like to confess, "I believe, therefore I have."  That means if I believe the way God taught me to believe in His Word (believe that what I say will come to pass), then I have what I desire.  Even if it's not instantly manifested, it is still already mine, by faith I already have it; I am just waiting for it to materialize. Just because I do not see it with my natural eyes doesn't mean I do not have it. I may not have it in the physical realm, but I still have it through my faith in God. So, all that is left for it to do is to take on natural shape and form; that is where patience comes in. James 1:4 says, **"But let patience have its perfect work, that you may be perfect and complete, <u>lacking nothing</u>."** Look back a few verses with me, to verses 28 & 29 in John 6.

**"Then they said to Him, "What shall we do, that we may work the works of God?"**
**Jesus answered and said to them, "This is the work of God, that you believe in Him whom He sent.""**

The people wanted to do the works of God, like we do today, so they asked Him how. He said the work of God is to <u>believe</u> in Him, or the work of God is just to believe. It's that simple! When you believe in Jesus as your Lord, then you just did the work of God. You now have eternal life, because believing is having. I hope you are getting a hold of this. It will set you free! It will give you a rest in your believing, no more stress! So, the work of God is to believe, and the first work we all get to do, is to believe in Jesus for salvation. That's just the first work of God; expect many, many more to come!

In John 11, Jesus went to raise Lazarus from the dead. When He was standing before the tomb of his friend, He told them to take away the stone. Then in verse 40, He said to Martha, **"Did I not say to you that if <u>you</u> would believe <u>you</u> would <u>see</u> the glory of God?"** The saying of the world is seeing is believing, but that is not correct. Jesus said if you believe you will see. You have to believe first! Faith in God always comes first; then you get to feel the miracle and see the miracle! If we will believe, then we will see the glory of God! What is the glory of God? The Greek word for glory is doxa. It means the majestic, absolute perfection residing in Christ and evidenced by the miracles He performed. The glory of God can be manifested as a cloud that fills the temple. Also, when Jesus turned the water into wine, that was a manifestation of His glory according to John 2:11. Of course when He raised Lazarus from the dead; that was a demonstration of His glory. Whenever God saves, heals, delivers and works miracles for people, He is showing us His glory! When you lead someone to the Lord, you just saw God's glory! When you get someone healed in Jesus' Name, you just saw the Glory of God! You saw the glory of God when the job you prayed for came to pass. We are seeing God's glory more and more and more everywhere we go, because we believe! If you will just believe, you will see His glory to.

What do we need to believe? Again, Jesus told Martha in verse 11, **"Did I not say to you that if you would believe..."** He is referring to something He said to her before we read verse 11. What did He tell her to believe? Look at verses 25 & 26.

**"Jesus said to her, "I am the resurrection and the life. He who believes in Me, though he may die, he shall live.**

**And whoever lives and believes in Me shall never die. <u>Do you believe this</u>?"**

What Jesus told her to believe sounds a lot like what He told the people in John Chapter 6. Remember, He said the work of God is to believe in Him whom God has sent. Martha said she believed that He was the resurrection and the life, and that by believing on Him she would spiritually live forever. Well, according to what the Lord said in John Chapter 6, Martha just did the work of God. So, the first work of God (or the glory of God) that you get to see or experience, by operating in faith, is your salvation. Jesus said, **"...If you would believe you would see the glory of God."** When you believed on Jesus, you saw His glory in your salvation. You began your Christian life by doing the work of God, and it was the greatest of all miracles! Therefore, when Jesus told Martha, **"Did I not say to you..."**, He was telling her how she could see the glory of God by the raising of Lazarus from the dead. He wanted Martha, you and me to know that you operate in faith the same way to see His glory as you did to be saved.

Therefore, believing is having! If you believe, you have; then you will see God's glory or what you have. Every time you say or pray what you expect to come to pass, you will see His glory! Expect it! Again, the greatest glory we will ever see is the new birth. If you can believe God and see His glory there, then you can see His glory anywhere else! In John 15:7 & 8, the Lord Jesus said:

"If you abide in Me, and My words abide in you, you will ask what you desire, and it shall be done for you.

By this My Father is <u>glorified, that you bear much fruit</u>; so you will be My disciples."

God's way of bearing fruit through us comes when we exercise our faith to see His glory. Seeing His glory manifested through us is bringing glory to Him. Seeing His glory is seeing the fruit of our faith. Therefore, bearing fruit in our lives is glorifying God, which is seeing His glory.

As Leia and I travel and minister in churches, we are seeing more healings and miracles among the people. I believe that a New Testament church or a Word and Spirit church is a place where the uncompromised Word of God is taught, and demonstrated in the Spirit and power of God (I Corinthians 2:4). It's a place where the Gifts of the Spirit and the glory of God are manifested. We minister a lot through the laying on of hands, but we also have services where the people will receive without us touching them. We expect the power gifts (gifts of healings, gift of faith and the working of miracles-I Corinthians 12:4-11) to be in operation in our meetings. So, many times after we have taught the Word, we will have all those who need healing or a miracle in their bodies to stand up. We will then remind them that releasing their faith is just a decision they make, and they can do that right now. We also remind them that God's power to save, heal and deliver is available because of the Word we just preached.

We explain to the people that if they would make the decision (right now) to believe the Word they heard, then that power would go into them and heal their bodies in Jesus' Name!  It's just that simple!  After we release our faith to God, we then begin to praise and thank Him for all of the healings and miracles.  Then we take a moment to hear testimonies from all of those who are already experiencing healing in their bodies.  It's almost humorous to see the looks on some of the faces of those who seemed surprised that their healing came to pass.  It's as if they thought it can't be that easy.  Yes I know what you are probably thinking, not everyone will be healed instantly.  I am aware of that, but that still should not stop us from expecting more and more instant healings and miracles in Jesus' Name!  In Mark 16:17, 18, the Lord Jesus said that Believers would lay hands on the sick and they would recover!  Recover means, if it doesn't happen immediately then it will come to pass over the process of time.

Here are two testimonies from a church we ministered in.  We ministered there on a Wednesday night and the pastor said these 2 testimonies came in the following Sunday.  He said one man was suffering shoulder pain after having an episode on August 2, 2014 and going to the doctor and enduring several tests.  The pain left his shoulder by the next day (after being ministered to in the service Wednesday night) and he underwent a treadmill stress test and had to run uphill on it for 12 minutes to get his heart rate up to 146.  They told him no one had ever lasted 12 minutes on the treadmill before.  His heart checked out clear.

Another woman was suffering something like carpal tunnel in her left hand.  She had come to the service with her hand in a brace and it had been virtually useless for the past three or four days.  She raised her hands as we directed and felt a tingling in both wrists and was completely well and able to use the hand normally the next day.  She had sought prayer for the condition on more than one occasion before Wednesday and was even a bit skeptical as she raised her hands, but knew immediately that God was working in her body.  To Jesus be the glory!

Let me say this one more time.  Operating in the spirit of faith is a demonstration of the simplicity of believing. I got to thinking one day about Abraham's faith.  We normally refer to him as the father of faith.  Romans 4:17-22 says:

**"(As it is written, "I have made you a father of many nations") in the presence of Him whom he believed-God, who gives life to the dead and calls those things which do not exist as though they did;**

**Who, contrary to hope, in hope believed, so that he became the father of many nations, according to what was spoken, "So shall your descendants be."**

**And not being weak in faith, he did not consider his own body, already dead (since he was about a hundred years old), and the deadness of Sarah's womb.**

**He did not waver at the promise of God through unbelief, but was strengthened in faith, giving glory to God,**

**And being fully convinced that what He had promised He was also able to perform.**

**And therefore "it was accounted to him for righteousness.""**

Now I want you to think about this with me. When Abraham believed God, he did not have a Bible, he did not have the Old Testament and he didn't have the book of Genesis. He did not have any books or cd's to teach him how to operate in faith. There were not any churches and there were no faith seminars to attend for training. Basically, he was on his own. He was alone. He probably had no minister friends to call for encouragement. When Almighty God came to him, Abraham had no children, not even one child. It was just him and his wife, not counting other relatives. The Lord spoke to him and said that He had made him the father of many nations. God told him this when he was probably around 75 years old, then when he was about 100 years old he had his son Isaac. What excites me is the greatness of his faith. Let me explain further. When God told him about this awesome miracle, not just having a son, but becoming the father of many nations, Abraham just believed it! It would have been stupendous to know you will be the father of one nation, but of many nations? That is truly awesome, but here is what may be just as awesome, Abraham believed it! The Bible did not say he argued with the Lord until God convinced him to believe. He just believed!

I have been talking about how quickly you and I can make a decision to believe, or to operate in faith. Once again, Abraham gave us the perfect example. God didn't tell him that He was about to bless him with three new camels. No! God told him something that was totally impossible for man! I would think it was beyond anything Abraham could imagine. I dare say most Christians would not have believed that! To add to that thought, Abraham was not even a Christian, not filled with the Holy Spirit, not in the New Covenant, he did not have the written Word and he did not have examples of other men who became fathers of many nations. It greatly impresses and encourages me to think of how easily Abraham believed God. He just made a decision to believe. No matter how ridiculous it sounded to his head. Even though he did not understand how God would bring His Word to pass, he still believed. You don't have to understand how God will bring your healing to pass, or will meet your needs, just believe that He will! Believe that what you have applied your faith for will come to pass in Jesus' Name! Don't change your believing! Keep thanking and praising the Lord until your miracles are manifested! Don't say, "I <u>am going</u> to believe that God will heal me!" Say, "I believe that I am already healed by the stripes of Jesus, and right now I believe in my heart that my healing will come to pass!"

We could look at other great men and women of God. Consider Noah, God told him he would flood the entire earth. It had never rained before. Think of how preposterous that would have sounded if you did not have faith in God. Like Abraham, Noah just made a decision to believe it. The Bible doesn't say he argued at all with God.  He did not ask the Lord for references or proof that what He said would happen.  He just believed!  Just like that!  Genesis 6:22 says, **"Thus Noah did; according to all that God commanded him, so he did."**  Think of Mary for a moment.  In Luke 1:31, the angel Gabriel came to her and said, **"And behold, you will conceive in your womb and bring forth a Son, and shall call His name Jesus."**  She then asked how she could have a child without knowing a man.  She knew it takes more than one person to do that.  After Gabriel explained to her how the Holy Spirit would come upon her and work a miracle within her, she then said this:

**"Behold the maidservant of the Lord!  Let it be to me according to your word."  And the angel departed from her."**

Right then, she decided to believe the message from God!  Again, think how utterly ridiculous that sounded to her.  She did not know a man by a sexual relationship, but she was still going to have a baby; and to top it all off, this baby would be the Son of God!  Did she tell the angel that she would need about six months to decide if she would believe that or not?  Did she ask for testimonies of other women who supernaturally had babies without knowing any men? No!  The Lord brought a word to Mary that was totally impossible for man, and what did she say? I believe it!  Wow!  That's impressive!  She was still a young girl, probably a teenager.  God did not say, "Mary, you will not be able to believe this Word until you get a degree in theology and have been walking with Me for at least 30 years." Even with a very limited understanding of spiritual things, Mary chose to believe God. When she said, "Let it be to me according to Your Word" that was another way of saying, "I believe and I expect it to come to pass!"

After reading about these awesome miracles and hearing of how these men and women just simply believed God, you would assume that more Christians would be encouraged in their believing, but it hasn't always been that way. Many Christians talk as if believing God for anything is extremely difficult and hard to do. I believe that we (the Church) must get back to the basics of simple faith in God! In Mark 10:15, the Lord said that we must receive the Kingdom of God as a little child. Children just believe what their parents tell them. They do not question it. They may say, "Why", but even though they do not fully understand what their parents tell them, they still believe it. As Believers, we need to get back to that with our Heavenly Father! Even though we do not understand all the intricacies of what God said, we can still believe it. Don't wait to you fully understand it all to choose to believe God! Remember, we are believers! It should not be difficult for us to believe our God! These are also things that I am constantly reminding myself. I think we all have had answers to prayers that seemed to take a long time to come to pass, and even though we did not understand why, we still must keep believing God and exercising our faith so it can grow stronger and stronger. Don't ever give up! Even if you are not bench pressing the amount you desire, keep exercising those muscles, because they will grow stronger. In I Thessalonians 3:10, the Apostle Paul said:

**"Night and day praying exceedingly that we may see your face and perfect what is lacking in your faith."**

Sometimes I will pray and ask the Lord to perfect anything that may be lacking in my faith. I want to be used by God in the greatest way He can use me, don't you? I want to use my faith to be the biggest blessing to others that I can be, don't you? So, let's learn a great lesson from these pioneers of faith! That lesson is, be quick to believe God! When you read God's Word, make up your mind, right then, to believe it! Don't look at the circumstances around you! Don't look at the wind and waves of the storm surrounding you! Look at Jesus, the living Word! Even if you don't see results immediately, keep saying to yourself, "The Word is working mightily in me! All things are possible for me through my faith in God! And I believe that the things I have declared by faith will come to pass in Jesus' Name! I will not turn my faith off! I will believe and trust God no matter what is going on around me! I have made up my mind; I will always walk and live by faith every day for the rest of my life!"

*Just Believe*

# CHAPTER 3

# IS WHAT YOU SAY IMPORTANT?

I want to look now at how important words are in releasing and developing our faith. Remember, the Lord Jesus said (Matthew 17:20 & Luke 17:6) if we had faith as a mustard seed, we would say. He was instructing us to plant or sow our faith like we would sow a seed in the ground. The main way we operate in faith is by saying or speaking God's Word. The Lord gave us a very important parable that every Christian should understand. In Luke 8:5, He said a sower went out to sow his seed. He describes the different ground the seed fell on, and then He explains the parable in verses 11-15.

**"Now the parable is this: The seed is the word of God.**

**Those by the wayside are the ones who hear; then the devil comes and takes away the word out of their hearts, lest they should believe and be saved.**

**But the ones on the rock are those who, when they hear, receive the word with joy; and these have no root, who believe for a while and in time of temptation fall away.**

**Now the ones that fell among thorns are those who, when they have heard, go out and are choked with cares, riches, and pleasures of life, and bring no fruit to maturity.**

**But the ones that fell on the good ground are those who, having heard the word with a noble and good heart, keep it and bear fruit with patience."**

The seed is God's Word.  He compares the good ground to a good heart; so the ground the Word is being sown in is the heart of man (not the physical heart, but the spirit of man).  This entire parable is about hearing the Word of God, and how we respond to the Word we hear.  You could say there were four different types of ground or hearts.  The Bible says the first person heard the Word and the devil stole it out of his heart.  That tells me that the Word must have gone into his heart when he heard it.  So how do we get God's Word into our hearts?  By hearing it.  Now, once you hear that Word and it goes into your heart, you have to decide if you will keep it or not; because the devil cannot steal it just because he wants to, you have to allow him access. If you submit to God and resist the devil in Jesus' Name, he will flee from you (James 4:7)!

The Lord Jesus said that you can have what you say as long as you believe in your heart that the things you say will be done. Listen very closely! He did not say that you can have anything you say. That is where so many people have missed it and left confused. They ran off saying that you can have anything you say, and Jesus did not say that in Mark 11:23! Look one more time at what He said.

**"For assuredly, I say to you, whoever says to this mountain, 'Be removed and be cast into the sea,' and does not doubt in his heart, but <u>believes that those things he says will be done</u>, he will have whatever he says."**

The only time you will have what you say is when <u>you believe in your heart</u> that what you say will come to pass. If you cannot believe it will come to pass, then it will not be manifested. Just saying it robotically (over and over) will not make it come to pass either. Like I said before, there is a very important contingency here. You have to believe!

You and I can confess outrageous things and talk a big talk, but it all boils down to this; do you really (before God) believe that what you are saying will come to pass? Do you honestly believe it will happen? Even if you don't, I still have some good news for you. The Bible tells you how you can increase your faith so you can believe. You need to begin sowing the Word of God into your heart. Romans 10:8 says, **"...The word is near you, in your mouth and in your heart..."** The Word has to be in both places to work for us. Having what you say is not based on how big your confession is; it's based on what you believe in your heart. The main way to sow or plant the Word in your heart is by saying it. But again, it is not by seeing how many times you can repeat the same confession. Here is the difference, when you confess who you are in Christ, say it like you believe it's true. Every time you confess the Word, confess it with an attitude of expectancy; like you believe something is going to change in your life!

I have shared this example before, but it fits in so well here I want to share it again. Whenever I eat a T-bone steak, I chew eat bite up before I swallow it. I don't chew eat piece of meat to be mechanical. Even though I will chew it a number of times, I am not counting the times. I am not chewing that piece of steak to be robotic or to reach a certain count of how many times I chew it. I'm chewing it because I enjoy it. I keep chewing it until I am ready to swallow it, but it is not because I reached a certain count in number. Now, if you and I are in a restaurant and we are both chewing on a piece of steak at the same time, others will not be able to tell by looking at us if we are chewing just to reach a specific number or for enjoyment. One of us could be doing that while the other is not. I may confess that I am the righteousness of God in Christ (II Corinthians 5:21), but I am not saying it to be mechanical (even though some Christians may be saying it that way). I am saying it because I am enjoying it (just like that steak)! I may just confess it one time or twenty times, I am not counting. What I want you to understand is, I keep saying it as long as it (spiritually) tastes good.

When it comes to eating a steak, I like to imagine that while I am chewing that piece of meat, all of the nutrients in it are going into my body and strengthening me. I believe that spiritually the same thing is true when declaring who you are in Christ. Confessing God's Word is like spiritually chewing a piece of meat. I believe that as I speak God's Word all of the spiritual nutrients (life, healing power, peace, joy etc…) are being released into every area of my life and greatly strengthening me, while building up my faith at the same time. In Philemon 6, Paul instructed us to declare every good thing in us in Christ. He said that when we did this our faith would become effective or energized. That is what I want, for my faith to be very effective, don't you?

Many years ago there was a lot of teaching on positive thinking. Positive thinking is important, it's better than negative thinking, but positive thinking is not enough to change your life and those around you. In Mark 9:23, Jesus said all things are possible to him who believes, not to him who just thinks positively, and not to him who just has a positive confession. All things are only possible to him who believes or has faith in God. Man's physical and mental powers are limited, but God's spiritual power is unlimited. Only our faith in God activates His supernatural power; that is why **ALL** things are possible to us if we believe! We think before we speak, therefore what we think will determine what we speak, but we will only have what we speak if we believe in our hearts that it will come to pass.

Once again in Matthew 17:20 and Luke 17:6, the Lord Jesus describes our faith as a seed we are to sow, and then He tells us how to sow it. He said if you had faith as a mustard seed you would say something. He did not say if you had faith as a seed you would think, or if you had faith as a seed you would desire. Now, thinking and desiring are important, but He said the way we plant our faith as a seed is by saying. We must speak the Word! Hebrews 11:3 says,

**"By faith we understand that the worlds were framed by the <u>word</u> of God, so that the things which are seen were not made of things which are visible."**

The worlds were framed by the word of God, not by the thoughts or desires of God. God spoke the worlds into existence. So, God released or sowed His faith as seed by saying what He believed would be manifested, and He had what he said. As His sons and daughters, we are to operate the same way. That is how we walk and live by faith. It is how we live and minister in the supernatural, resurrection realm of God. Jesus compared spiritual seed to natural seed. Just as the farmer sows or plants his corn seed into the ground of the earth, a Believer sows his faith like a seed into the ground of his heart by his confession. Sowing my faith as a seed is the same as sowing the Word of God into my heart. What is the purpose of my confession? It is one of the main ways to get the Word into my heart, so that I can say, "I now believe it". When I read the Scriptures that tell me who I am in Christ and who He is in me, and declare them, they go into my eyes and ears, and from there into my heart (ground).  Proverbs 4:20-22 says:

**"My son, give attention to my words; incline your ear to my sayings.**
**Do not let them depart from your eyes; keep them in the midst of your heart;**
**For they are life to those who find them, and health to all their flesh."**

The way to sow God's Word and to keep His Word in the midst of our hearts is by keeping it in our eyes and ears.  He did not just say eyes or ears.  He did not say pick one of the two.  We need to make it a daily habit to read the Word and to hear the Word.  Hearing the Word on CD and through teaching from ministers is very important, but the most important way for you to hear the Word is when it comes out of <u>your</u> mouth.  That is the best way for God's Word to register and be implanted in the ground of your heart.  Even though you can quote many Scriptures by memory, take more time to look at them in your Bible while you are confessing them, so that God's Word can go into your eyes as well as your ears.  Now, let me show you what happens when we sow the Word of God into our hearts.

**"And He said, "The kingdom of God is as if a man should scatter seed on the ground,**
**And should sleep by night and rise by day, and the seed should sprout and grow, he himself does not know how.**

**For the earth yields crops by itself: first the blade, then the head, after that the full grain in the head.**

**But when the grain ripens, immediately he puts in the sickle, because the harvest has come."** Mark 4:26-29.

The Kingdom of God means the rule of God, or where God rules. The Lord Jesus said that the Kingdom of God is within us (Luke 17:21). He also said that His Kingdom is about sowing seed in the ground. It is about seed time and harvest. Farmers understand this principle. As Christians, we need to understand it; it is how the Kingdom of God works. Many times Jesus used natural examples to illustrate spiritual truths. If you sow tomato seeds in your garden, you are going to reap tomatoes. Once you plant the seeds they will start growing. When you go to sleep at night and rise during the day, they continue to grow. You can go to the store, the park, to work and they will keep growing until they produce a harvest.

That is the way our faith works when we sow it as a seed by saying. When you confess you are healed in Jesus' Name, you are sowing the seed for a harvest of healing into the ground of your heart. As you continue to make that confession, you are not only sowing that seed into your heart, but you are also watering the seed that has already been sown. The seed will continue to grow until you reap a harvest of healing in your body. In verse 27, Jesus said, **"And should sleep by night and rise by day, and the seed should sprout and grow, <u>he himself does not know how."</u>**

I like knowing that even though I do not understand how tomato seeds can produce tomatoes, it still does. You may be thinking, "I feel terrible in my body, so how does confessing by Jesus' stripes I am healed help me feel better?" Even if you do not understand how God's healing power is released into your body by believing and confessing His Word, it still works. <u>The life of the seed is in the seed</u>. The tomato harvest is in the tomato seeds. A seed cannot bear fruit but of its own kind.

**"Then God said, "Let the earth bring forth grass, the herb that yields seed, and the fruit tree that yields fruit according to its kind, <u>whose seed is in itself</u>, on the earth."** (Genesis 1:11)

The seed contains all that it needs to produce a harvest. We not only need to think of words as seed but also as containers. The Word of God contains everything it needs to produce that Word. Hebrews 4:12 tells us that God's Word (Seed) is alive and powerful. Hebrews 1:3 says that God upholds all things by the Word of His power, and John 1:1 says that the Word was with God and the Word was God. All that God is and has, all of His resources and power are in His Word! God put His healing power in His Word and you do not have to understand how it can come out of that Word and produce healing in your body. You get to reap the harvest of healing, prosperity, salvation, deliverance, joy, protection and peace, whether you know how it works or not! **"He sent His word and healed them, and** delivered them from their destructions." (Psalm107:20)

Mark 4:26 said, **"...As if a <u>man</u> should scatter seed on the ground."** Who sows the seed? Man sows the seed, not God. God doesn't confess for me that Jesus is my peace, I must do that. God will not go out and sow seed in your garden, you have to. God makes the seed work, but you must plant it! Jesus said that we have to speak to the mountain. The mountain is whatever is in your way or hindering you from doing what God wants you to do. It could be sickness, a demon, financial debt, fear, or whatever the devil is bringing against you. Jesus did not tell us to pray for God to speak to the mountain. We must talk to the mountain. He told us to plant our faith like a seed by saying, let's never forget that!

Remember, the kind of seed you sow will determine the kind of harvest you reap. <u>Your harvest is in your seed</u>. It is not in what you want or think. What you want and what you think are not your seed. <u>What you **say** is your seed</u>. A farmer doesn't harvest what he wants or what he thinks, only what he sows. If you do not want corn, then don't sow corn seed. If you want to be healed and walk in perfect health, then quit confessing you are sick and always in pain. Please listen very closely! You and I will only reap what we sow, <u>not what we want</u>! You may desire to never have the flu again, but as long as you keep confessing that you get it every year, your harvest will come from what you are saying and not from what you desire. You may want some cucumbers, but if all you plant are watermelon seeds, then guess what you will reap? You may desperately desire to pay all your bills and have plenty left over to bless others, but if you always say, "I am so broke. I don't know how I will ever make ends meet. With my luck I will probably lose my job", what do you think will come to pass in your life?  <u>The ground does not care what you want to eat or what you are thinking about eating</u>; it only cares what kind of seed that you plant in it.  Even in the natural realm, the ground will try to grow whatever you put in it, whether tomato seeds or weeds.  You could say that the ground is not a respecter of seeds.

Constantly confessing negative words over your children or any family members will not produce positive results in their lives!  If you want your children to be wise, mature, God fearing Christians, then quit saying that they are no good, rebellious children and will probably end up in jail.  Speaking negative words about your children, marriage, job, and even our country, is like wanting watermelons from your garden but planting cucumber seeds.  If you want your family members to be born again and to serve the Lord with all of their hearts, then start sowing the corresponding seeds; start confessing the Word of God over them, and don't turn your faith off no matter how they talk or act.  Let me say it one more time.  What you want for your life and family is not the seed your harvest will come from.  You may want God to do wonderful and good things in all of your lives, but if you don't start saying it and believing what you're saying will come to pass, then you will never have it.  Good intentions and Godly desires are not enough.  In the natural realm and in the spiritual realm, seed must be sown for a harvest to be reaped. What it boils down to is, many Christians want a harvest of what they desire in their hearts, but they are only getting a harvest from what they say, and many times, what they say is not in agreement with what they truly desire. Their harvest will only come out of the seed they sow, and what they desire is not their seed, what they say is their seed. Great power can be released through our words to bless or curse our lives. Let me share with you a few Scriptures about the power of words or you could say the power of the tongue.

**"A man's stomach shall be satisfied from the fruit of his mouth; from the produce of his lips he shall be filled.**
**Death and life are in the power of the tongue, and those who love it will eat its fruit."** (Proverbs 18:20, 21)

**"Words satisfy the mind as much as fruit does the stomach; good talk is as gratifying as a good harvest.**
**Words kill, words give life; they're either poison or fruit-you choose."**
(Proverbs 18:20, 21- Message Bible)

James 3: 3-8 says:
**"Indeed, we put bits in horses' mouths that they may obey us, and we turn their whole body.**
**Look also at ships: although they are so large and are driven by fierce winds, they are turned by a very small rudder wherever the pilot desires.**

Even so the tongue is a little member and boasts great things. See how great a forest a little fire kindles!

And the tongue is a fire, a world of iniquity. The tongue is so set among our members that it defiles the whole body, and sets on fire the course of nature; and it is set on fire by hell.

For every kind of beast and bird, of reptile and creature of the sea, is tamed and has been tamed by mankind.

But no man can tame the tongue. It is an unruly evil, full of deadly poison."

I know it is a lot of Scriptures, but I want you to see these same verses out of the Message Bible.

"A bit in the mouth of a horse controls the whole horse. A small rudder on a huge ship in the hands of a skilled captain sets a course in the face of the strongest winds. A word out of your mouth may seem of no account, but it can accomplish nearly anything- or destroy it!

It only takes a spark, remember, to set off a forest fire. A careless or wrongly placed word out of your mouth can do that. By our speech we can ruin the world, turn harmony to chaos, throw mud on a reputation, send the whole world up in smoke and go up in smoke with it, smoke right from the pit of hell.

This is scary: You can tame a tiger, but you can't tame a tongue- it's never been done. The tongue runs wild, a wanton killer."

The one thing man cannot tame is his tongue, but the Holy Spirit can. When you yield (everyday) your spirit, soul (will, intellect and emotions) and body (including your tongue) to the Holy Spirit and allow Him to flow freely in your life, allow Him to have His way, not your way; then He will help you to control your tongue so that it lines up with God's Word. That is why it's so important, as we read earlier in Proverbs 4, to put the Word in our eyes and ears each day. That's how we get it into our hearts, so we can believe what we say will come to pass. The Lord Jesus said that out of the abundance of the heart, the mouth speaks (Matthew 12:34). What is in people's hearts will come out of their mouths, whether good or bad; let's make it good. The pressure from tests and trials will always reveal what is in people's hearts. If I need to know what is truly in a person's heart, then I need to be around him when the pressure comes. A person may be able to "fake" a good confession when his circumstances are pleasant, but the truth of what has been sown his heart will be made known when his circumstances turn negative. The pressures of life help each one of us to see how established we are in God's Word. Let's make every effort to stay full of the Word of God!

# CHAPTER
4

# LIVING IN SUPERNATURAL PEACE

It's easy to say we live in peace when we are not under attack, but when the tests come we will find out if our faith is working. If we are truly in faith we will be in perfect peace, no matter what happens around us. I did not say we will like everything that happens, but we will stay in peace. Our peace doesn't come from good circumstances. It comes from Jesus within us! I want you to listen to something Jesus said to the church in Smyrna.

**"Do not fear any of those things which you are about to suffer. Indeed, the devil is about to throw some of you into prison, that you may be tested, and you will have tribulation ten days. Be faithful until death, and I will give you the crown of life."** (Revelation 2:10)

This was a prophecy the Lord spoke to these Believers. It wasn't what we would call a good and exciting Word from the Lord. I don't know anyone who would hope for a prophecy like that. They could not dismiss it by saying, "Men make mistakes. Sometimes they do not hear accurately. Maybe this word will not come to pass." It was not just a man who prophesied this. It was God Himself. Now Jesus cannot lie and He cannot miss it, and He told them they would suffer for ten days in prison and then be killed. He did not say they would suffer and then be delivered, and live the rest of their lives in joy and prosperity. I don't know what their situation in life was at that time, but the Lord knew their futures. He knew what was going to happen to them. He did not comfort them by saying that these things might not happen to them. He simply told them not to be afraid. Now, He would not have told them that if they could not do it. He let them know that they could be at peace (inside) even though they were about to give up their lives. I believe this will help us to better understand what the Lord said in John 14:27.

**"Peace I leave with you, My peace I give to you; not as the world gives do I give to you. Let not your heart be troubled, neither let it be afraid."**

He said that He left His peace with us. He gave us His peace. What we need to do is accept that by faith. The peace of Jesus is different than the peace from the world. The world's peace is based on the circumstances around us. If things are good, the people are at peace.

If things are bad, the people are afraid and depressed. Their peace comes from the outside, what is going on around them. Our peace comes from within. It is a peace we can experience even when everything around us is in turmoil! We can be at peace right in the middle of the storms of life! Why? Because of what Jesus told us in John 16:33.

**"These things I have spoken to you, that <u>in Me you may have peace</u>. In the world you will have tribulation; but be of good cheer, I have overcome the world."**

Jesus came right out and said that we would have tribulation in this world. He did not sugar coat it, but He still told us to rejoice. Why? Because He has overcome this world we live in. Since He has overcome it, and we are in Him, then we have overcome it and have His peace. His peace fills us through His presence abiding within us. No matter what tribulations we may face, we can do it fearlessly in the peace of God if we stay in faith. Yet, it's not an automatic thing. You can experience the peace the world gives if you so choose and you will be emotionally up and down like a roller coaster every day.

Jesus instructed us on how to release our faith to experience His continual peace, at the end of John 14:27. He said, **"Let not your heart be troubled, neither let it be afraid."** This was a command to you and me. He did not say, "<u>Try</u> not to let your heart be troubled…" He just said to do it! Remember, we release our faith like a seed by saying. It works the same way to experience God's peace. We need to declare, "Because

Jesus is my peace, I will not let my heart be troubled or afraid! It doesn't matter what I am dealing with in life, I will live every day at rest and at peace in Christ Jesus. He is always the same; therefore, He is always my peace. I will not let my heart be stressed or worried about anything! My mind is at peace. My body is at peace. I have the peace of God all of the time! I am not moved by what I see or hear from others! I am only moved by what I believe! I believe God's Word! I believe and therefore have. So, I expect to see the glory of God manifested in my life and all around me in Jesus' Name!" I don't know about you, but that gives me peace by just saying that. I am going to keep believing it and saying it the rest of my life!

When Peter was put in prison in Acts 12, he was not afraid. Herod had just killed James with the sword and seized Peter as well. How do we know that Peter was not afraid and was at peace? Acts 12:6 says, "And when Herod was about to bring him out, that night Peter was sleeping, bound with two chains between two soldiers; and the guards before the door were keeping the prison." How could he be sleeping the night before his possible execution? Peter's faith in God and perfect peace had nothing to do with his outward circumstances, did it? He knew that Jesus was His peace, and refused to let his heart be troubled or afraid, even though he was fully aware that in the morning he might be the next martyr for the Church. I think many Christians believe that the reason why they can resist fear and be at peace is because they know there is a light at the end of the tunnel. They know there circumstances are going to get better at some point, so they try to hang in there and stay at peace until the things around them change.

For these Christians in Smyrna, there was not any light at the end of the tunnel in this life, but they could look forward to a crown of life awaiting them in the next life. The Apostle Peter did not know that an angel would deliver him. He did not have any advanced notice to encourage him to stay in peace until the next morning. He was so asleep the angel had to strike him on the side to wake him up. In Mark 4, Jesus took a nap in the middle of a storm, while their boat was filling up with water. That is supernatural peace! We have that kind of peace in Christ! It has nothing to do with the tests and trials we may be facing right now in our lives! So, stand up boldly on God's Word and declare, "I will not let my heart be worried, troubled or afraid because Jesus is my peace and He always causes me to triumph in all things (II Corinthians 2:14)!!"

Please let me remind you of the story of Shadrach, Meshach and Abednego in Daniel chapter 3. King Nebuchadnezzar built an image of gold that was about 90 feet tall. He said when the music begins to play; everyone must bow down and worship before this idol. Verse 6 says, **"And whoever does not fall down and worship shall be cast immediately into the midst of a burning fiery furnace."** The three Hebrew young men chose not to do that because they worshipped God and Him alone. In Verses 17 & 18, they told the king that whether he cast them into the furnace or not, they would not worship the gold image. They said our God will deliver us from your hand, O king. The king commanded that the furnace be heated seven times more than it was usually heated. When the king's men cast Shadrach, Meshach and Abednego into the furnace, the flame of the fire killed those men. Do you want to talk about tests and trials? These young men were facing a major test and trial, but they were still at peace. Even though they were in faith, they were still thrown into the furnace. In this case, their faith in God did not get rid of the furnace. Please remember, just because you are in faith does not mean you will not face difficulties. But listen to what happened.

**"And these three men, Shadrach, Meshach, and Abed-Nego, fell down bound into the midst of the burning fiery furnace.**

**Then King Nebuchadnezzar was astonished; and he rose in haste and spoke, saying to his counselors, "Did we not cast three men bound into the midst of the fire?" They answered and said to the king, "True, O king."**

**"Look!" he answered, "I see four men loose, walking in the midst of the fire; and they are not hurt, and the form of the fourth is like the Son of God."** (Daniel 3:23-25)

When they came out of the fire, verse 27 says, **"And the satraps, administrators, governors, and the king's counselors gathered together, and they saw these men on whose bodies the fire had no power; the hair of their head was not singed nor were their garments affected, and the smell of fire was not on them."**

I believe that many Christians have the idea that the removal of the fire, test or negative circumstance is proof that their faith is working. The devil tells them that their faith is not working as long as their situation has not changed for the better. That is not always true. If that were true in the story we just read, then these three young men that God delivered would not have had any faith. If they were not in faith, they would have been burnt to ashes. After they were thrown in the fire, God did not turn the fire off. They were not immediately taken out of the furnace. They did some walking around in there. The king saw them walking in the <u>midst</u> of the fire. They were not in another room looking at the fire through a window. They were in the middle of it. Their problem was all around them. Have you ever felt that way? Have you ever felt surrounded by the enemy (the devil) and what he is doing? Surrounded by debt, sickness and disease, fear, depression, losing your job, marital problems, people lying about you and things not going your way?

A great revelation I want you to see is that God protected and met the needs of these three young men while they were in the fire. In other words, God didn't have to get rid of the fire to meet their needs! He didn't have to change their circumstances to take care of them. They were just as free in the fire as they were out of the fire! The Bible says they were not burned and did not even have the smell of smoke! Wow! There was not any evidence on them that they had been in the fire! When we trust Jesus as our peace, God as our one and only source, and refuse to allow our hearts to be troubled and afraid; He will protect and prosper us, no matter what is coming against us!  We will live every day in peace and supernatural joy whether we are in or out of the furnace of life!  We can expect our Heavenly Father to turn around every situation to work out for our good and His glory (Romans 8:28)!

The same thing happened to Isaac in Genesis chapter 26.  The only difference was, instead of being in the midst of a fire, he was in the midst of a famine.  The Bible said that he sowed his seed in the ground while in a famine, and he reaped a hundredfold return while still in the famine.  First of all, he did not use the famine or a bad economy as an excuse not to plant or give.  Because he was faithful in his sowing or you could say giving, God was faithful to make sure he reaped a great harvest.  Whether there was a famine or not, God met his need.  Whether we are in the middle of some kind of tribulation or not, God will meet all our need if we trust and obey Him.  Of course, we want the tribulation to go away, but we need to know that God will take care of us the whole time we are in it!  That means your faith is working all of the time, whether you are under immediate attack or no threat of attack; so God's peace should be what we continue to live in from day to day!

To become successful at this, we cannot allow the devil to steal the Word (Seed) of God out of our hearts.  Once again, in the parable of the sower, Jesus said that Satan comes immediately to take away the Word that was sown in the person's heart.  How does he do that?  He can't just take the Word out of our hearts because he wants to.  He has to trick us into opening up a door for him to do that. He has to convince us to dig up our seed, so to speak. The Lord said he does it through tribulations coming into our lives. In Mark 4:17, Jesus said, **"...When tribulation or persecution arises for the word's sake, immediately they stumble."** The devil knows that if the Word remains in the ground of our hearts, it will start growing and finally produce a harvest. When he comes against you with negative circumstances, he is trying to get you to dig up your seed. In the verse we just read the word "stumble" also means to be offended. If you get mad (offended) because your healing has not come to pass, and start confessing, "I guess this didn't work. I guess my faith doesn't work for healing. I tried, but it doesn't look like my healing will come to pass." The devil just caused you to stumble. When you get offended, that is another way of saying you just stumbled. You fell right into his trap and enabled him to steal the Word out of your heart. Now, he could not do that unless you gave him permission with your mouth. The devil could spend an entire day saying that your healing will not come to pass, but that would not override your confession of faith or the seed that you sowed. Let's stay so full of God's Word we will always recognize the devil's strategies and not fall for them!

Think about this with me. If a farmer planted green beans on his property, he would not go out in a couple of days and dig up the seed because he has not seen any sign of green beans coming up. Even if there is a bad storm and he has doubts about his harvest coming forth, he will still leave the seed in the ground and wait patiently to see what happens. When you make up your mind to start speaking God's Word over yourself, family members, etc... maintain your confession of faith no matter how the circumstances look! If the circumstances seem worse after you release your faith, don't be discouraged. Those negative circumstances are not proof that your faith is not working. If you are serving God with all of your heart and living by faith, then <u>conflict is a sign that you are progressing</u>! Don't let the devil deceive you into turning off your faith. If you start speaking contrary to God's Word regarding your faith confessions, it is the same as going out to your garden and digging up your seed. It will never grow that way! You planted your seed with your mouth; you can dig it up the same way. Now listen! You are the only one who can dig up your faith seed, and the devil knows that. He knows that he cannot turn off your faith. The devil's only strategy is to manipulate things in the world around you, in hopes that you will negate your confession, thereby digging up your seed. He is hoping that you will take your eyes off of Jesus and think about how your body feels or about how many bills you have, but he does not want you to stand unwavering for the manifestation of your harvest.

If the devil or people tell me that my healing will not come to pass, my financial miracles will not come to pass, my children will never serve God or anything else contrary to what I am believing God for, I don't listen to them! What they say or do cannot stop my seed from growing! For me, it is about what I say, not what other people say! What I confess over my life is more powerful than what other people confess over my life!

**"No weapon formed against you shall prosper, and every tongue which rises against you in judgment you shall condemn. This is the heritage of the servants of the Lord, and their righteousness is from Me, says the Lord."** (Isaiah 54:17)

If the devil and all of his witches come together and start confessing evil against me, it will not condemn what I am confessing in Jesus' Name! It will not destroy or stop what I am declaring from coming to pass! But what I speak and prophesy from God's holy Word will condemn and totally destroy their confessions against me! What I say in the Name of the Lord will render powerless and ineffective the weapon of words they are bringing against me!! As God's righteousness in Christ, this is our heritage, and the devil cannot take it from us! Let me say it one more time. If someone comes to me every day and tells me that the tomato seeds I planted will never produce any tomatoes, I would not listen to a word they say! No matter how many times they declare that my tomato seeds will only produce cucumbers, I will still reap a tomato harvest! Nothing and no one can override my confession of faith! The devil cannot reverse God's blessing in my life! The devil cannot stop me from sowing the seed of God's Word in the ground of my heart, and he cannot stop it from growing and producing my harvest. He knows that, and every Believer needs to know that. So, start recognizing his strategy when you release your faith for things, and don't give in to his tricks. Don't dig up your seed! Leave it in the ground and let it grow! Again, Mark 4:28 & 29 says:

**"For the earth yields crops by itself: first the blade, then the head, after that the full grain in the head.**
**But when the grain ripens, immediately he puts in the sickle, because the harvest has come."**

When the ground produces a harvest, it is first the blade, then the head, after that the full grain in the head, then you have reaped your harvest. We should always keep expecting more things to come to pass instantly in Jesus' Name, but if they do not, don't give up on your faith, keep it applied by keeping your seed in the ground. You may be confessing for weeks or months that your back is healed; then one morning you wake up and realize that your back feels better, maybe not 100%, but better. That is the blade that just came up! About three days later when you get up you are startled because you can bend over better. That is the head that just came up! A week later, you are walking into a store and it dawns on you that all the pain has left your body and your back feels great. That is the full grain in the head! What does that mean? That means you put the sickle in and reaped the full harvest of your healing. You allowed the seed of your confession of faith to stay in the ground until it could grow and produce what you desired, which was healing. Faith in God works the same way in every area of our lives. Once again, I know that what you desire is important, but just desiring the blessings of God manifested in your life is not enough.

Begin sowing seed in your ground everyday by confessing, **"The blessing of the Lord makes one rich and He adds no sorrow with it (Proverbs 10:22). I am a brand new creation in Christ. I am the blessed of the Lord. The same blessing that was on Adam, Abraham and Jesus is on me, and that blessing has made me rich (fully supplied) in every area of my life. I am not only blessed, but I am a great blessing to others in Jesus' Name! Everywhere I go each day, I go in the fullness of the blessing of the Gospel of Christ (Romans 15:29)!"** Whenever I say that, I am sowing it as seed into the ground of my heart, and it will work day and night to bring that to pass in my life. And now, I have learned enough over the years not to dig up my seed. Therefore, it gives me great peace to know the Word I have been declaring (or prophesying) is working mightily in my life and for my family while I am sleeping at night. It never stops working for me! Even God's angels are working for me to bring to pass what I am saying! Psalm 103:20 says:

**"Bless the Lord, you His angels, who excel in strength, who do His word, <u>heeding the voice of His word</u>."**

The angels heed the voice of His Word. Who is putting voice to God's Word? I am, by my confession of faith. He did not say the angels heed the <u>thoughts</u> of His Word. God's angels listen to and obey His Word that <u>I</u>

speak. So, it is not just me they are listening to. They are listening to any Christian who will give voice to the Word of God. The angels only obey God's Word that we speak or put in our mouths. Angels are sent to minister for those who will inherit salvation (Hebrews 1:14).

According to Romans 4:17, when we put our voice to God's Word, when we speak what we believe will come to pass (before it has), then we are calling those things which be not (be not manifested) as though were. It is the same as calling those things which do not exist as though they did.

**"(As it is written, "I have made you a father of many nations") in the presence of Him whom he believed-God, who gives life to the dead and calls those things which do not exist as though they did."**

Once again, God told Abraham (before he even had a son) that he was the father of many nations. He did not say that Abraham <u>would be</u> the father of many nations. He said it as though it was already manifested in the natural realm. He said right now you are the father of many nations. You may be thinking, "Well that was a lie". Wait minute. The Bible says it is impossible for God to lie. God's Word is Truth (John 17:17)! That means whatever God says is true. It's true before we perceive it with our natural senses. Our natural senses do not make things true; they simply enable us to contact this physical world. Here is where the world and many Christians have messed up. They think that what they see, hear and touch is the only thing that is true, but that form of evidence only connects them with the physical realm. They need to understand that the spiritual realm is more real than the physical realm. God always takes the things that are real and true in the spiritual realm and brings them to pass in the physical realm.

**"By faith we understand that the worlds were framed by the word of God, so that the things which are seen were not made of things which are visible."** (Hebrews 11:3)

So, seeing the fruit of our faith is not when it becomes true. Your body may tell you that you are sick, but that is a lie when you compare it to Truth. God's Word says you are healed (I Peter 2:24). Your physical senses may tell you that you are sick, but all they can identify are natural facts. You are not denying how you feel. You just choose not to walk by your feelings. Yes, it is a fact (in the natural realm) that your body is in pain, but Truth says you are healed by Jesus' stripes! If you will believe and confess God's Truth, it will supersede and override the natural facts and change them to come into agreement with Truth!    Remember what we said earlier that asking is receiving?  Think about that now with Mark 11:24, **"...Whatever things you ask when you pray, believe that you receive them, and you will have them."**   Believing you receive the things you desire when you pray, means they are yours. They are yours as soon as you ask, not when they come to pass. When they come to pass is simply when your natural senses perceive them. That is not when they became yours. That is when they were transported by God's power out of the spiritual realm into the natural realm. Therefore asking is receiving. Seeking is finding. Believing is having.

Let's go back to Romans 4:17. The Bible said that God gives life to the dead and calls those things which do not exist as though they did. Abraham and Sarah's bodies were dead for having children (Romans 4:19-he was about 100 years old). How did God make their bodies alive again? He called those things which be not (this is how it reads in the King James Bible) as though they were. He said, "Abraham, you are a father of many nations." It wasn't just God's confession; Abraham said the same thing every time he told someone his name. Remember, words are containers. They can contain faith, life, and power. Every time he called those things which be not as though they were, the life and power of God was released into their bodies until their harvest came to pass. God wants to give life, healing, deliverance, prosperity and miracles to people through the words of our mouths.

In second Kings Chapter four, God prophesied through Elisha to a Shunammite woman that she would have a child. She did not have any sons and her husband was old, but God gave them a supernatural miracle. The child began to grow and one day he was outside and complained about his head hurting. Verses 20-23 say:

**"When he had taken him and brought him to his mother, he sat on her knees till noon, and then died.**

**And she went up and laid him on the bed of the man of God, shut the door upon him, and went out.**

**Then she called to her husband, and said, "Please send me one of the young men and one of the donkeys, that I may run to the man of God and come back."**

**So he said, "Why are you going to him today? It is neither the New Moon nor the Sabbath." And she said, "It is well.""**

Was everything well? No, not naturally speaking. Her son was dead. All of her physical senses bore witness to that fact, but is there something higher and truer than natural facts? She did not say that everything is going to be well. She said that it is well now! Her son is dead and she is saying that everything is fine. What is that called? That is called saying those things which be not as though they were, why? So they can become. Become what? Manifested! She expected to use her natural senses to see her son alive and well, but she had to first operate in faith for God to bring it to pass. Elisha told his servant Gehazi, in verse 26,

**"Please run now to meet her, and say to her, 'Is it well with you? Is it well with your husband? Is it well with the child?'" And she answered, "It is well.""** God was using her to give life to her son through her confession of faith. God used Elisha, but she was the one who called those things which do not exist as though they did. Because she believed what she said would come into existence (in the natural realm) before it did exist, enabled the Lord to use the prophet in raising her son from the dead.

**"When Elisha came into the house, there was the child, lying dead on his bed.**

**He went in therefore, shut the door behind the two of them, and prayed to the Lord.**

**And he went up and lay on the child, and put his mouth on his mouth, his eyes on his eyes, and his hands on his hands; and he stretched himself out on the child, and the flesh of the child became warm.**

**He returned and walked back and forth in the house, and again went up and stretched himself out on him; then the child sneezed seven times, and the child opened his eyes."** (II Kings 4:32-35)

The Lord Jesus said that He came to give us abundant life (John 10:10) and the main way He did that for the people was by calling those things which be not as though they were. In John 6:63, Jesus said, **"...The words that I speak to you are spirit, and they are life."** He was constantly releasing the life of God and healing, miracle working power into the people by calling them healed before they were, by telling them to rise and walk before they could, by telling Lazarus to come forth before he appeared in the entrance of the tomb, by commanding demons to leave before they left and by commanding the wind and waves to be at peace before they were! That is calling those things which be not as though they were!

The prophet Isaiah said:

**"For as the rain comes down, and the snow from heaven, and do not return there, but water the earth, and make it bring forth and bud, that it may give seed to the sower and bread to the eater,**

**So shall My word be that goes forth from My mouth; It shall not return to Me void, but it shall accomplish what I please, and it shall prosper in the thing for which I sent it.**" (Isaiah 55:11**)**

God compares His Word to rain and snow coming down and watering the earth. The water is giving life to the plants on the earth. God said my Word is like that when it goes out of His mouth. How does God's Word go forth from His mouth? Through you and me. We are His mouth on this earth. We are His voice to this world. When we call those things which be not as though they were, it is like the rain coming down on the earth. Salvation, healing, resurrection life and the blessings of Heaven are being imparted through us into this earth; especially into all of the people we prophecy to and pray for in Jesus' Name. Remember, Jesus said that the Kingdom of God is as if a man should sow seed on the ground. As soon as he does, the seed will start growing to produce a harvest, meaning it will not return void, as long as you leave it in the ground! I challenge you from this day forward to guard the words of your mouth and don't flippantly say things! Don't speak contrary to God's Word, because when you do, you are speaking against Truth! Truth is a person. His Name is Jesus (John 14:6). Every time we speak God's Word and declare who we are in Christ, we are glorifying the Lord!

We are releasing and planting our faith like a seed by our confession so that all things will be possible for us! I want to bless you with this verse in Ephesians 4:29.

**"Let no corrupt word proceed out of your mouth, but what is good for necessary edification, that it may <u>impart grace to the hearers.</u>"**

What we say isn't only important for us, but for those around us. When we speak God's Word, He will actually impart His grace (the operation of His power and favor) through us to others! Our Heavenly Father has blessed us to be a blessing, so let's be the biggest blessing we can be to others every day and everywhere we go! We are the blessed of the Lord, and to our God be all the glory!!

# About the Author

Dwayne Norman is a 1978 graduate of Christ For The Nations Bible Institute in Dallas, Texas. He spent 3 years witnessing to prostitutes and pimps in the red light district of Dallas, and another 3 years ministering as a team leader in the Campus Challenge ministry of Dr. Norvel Hayes. He was ordained by Pastor Buddy and Pat Harrison of Faith Christian Fellowship in Tulsa, Oklahoma in September 1980. He also taught evangelism classes several times at Dr. Hayes' Bible school in Tennessee.

Soon the Lord led him to go on the road ministering. He ministers powerfully on soul winning, and on how God wants to use all Believers in demonstrating His Kingdom not just in Word but also in Power!

He teaches with clarity, the work that God accomplished for all believers in Christ from the cross to the throne, and the importance of this revelation to the church for the fulfillment of Jesus' commission to make disciples of all nations.

He strongly believes that we are called to do the works Jesus did and greater works in His Name, not just in church but especially in the market place. As a result Dwayne experiences many healing miracles in his services, arms and legs growing out, as well as other miracles.

He and his wife Leia travel and teach Supernatural Evangelism and train Believers in who they are in Christ and how to operate in their ministries.

**To inquire for meetings with Dwayne & Leia Norman, please contact them at:**

Dwayne & Leia Norman
124 Evergreen Court
Mt. Sterling, KY 40353

(859) 351-6496
dwayne7@att.net
Web: www.dwaynenormanministries.org

**Contact Dwayne to order his other books and products:**

| | |
|---|---|
| The Mystery DVD's (12 hours) | $50.00 |
| The Mystery (book) | $12.00 |
| The Mystery Study Guide | $10.00 |
| The Awesome Power in the Message of the Cross | $10.00 |
| Your Beginning with God | $10.00 |
| The Law of the Spirit of Life in Christ Jesus | $10.00 |
| Demonstrating God's Kingdom | $10.00 |

www.ingramcontent.com/pod-product-compliance
Lightning Source LLC
Chambersburg PA
CBHW060036050426
42448CB00012B/3035